The Nation's #1 Educational Publisher

The McGraw·Hill Companies

The McGraw·Hill Junior Academic Series

Toddler My 1,2,3's

Numbers & Counting

A McGraw·Hill/Warner Bros. Workbook

Table of Contents

Credits:
McGraw-Hill Learning Materials Editorial/Production Team
Vincent F. Douglas, B.S. and M. Ed.
Tracy R. Paulus
Jennifer P. Blashkiw

Design Studio
Mike Legendre; Creativity On Demand

Warner Bros. Worldwide Publishing Editorial/Production Team
Michael Harkavy
Paula Allen
Victoria Selover
Charles Carney
Allen Helbig

Illustrators
Cover and Interior: Arkadia Illustration & Design—London

McGraw-Hill
Consumer Products
A Division of The McGraw-Hill Companies

Published by McGraw-Hill Learning Materials, an imprint of McGraw-Hill Consumer Products.

Send all inquiries to:
McGraw-Hill Consumer Products
250 Old Wilson Bridge Road
Worthington, Ohio 43085

1-57768-218-1

NAME ______________________________

ONE

1

1

Directions: Using the top half of the page, show your child the number 1. Explain that Baby Bugs is holding *one* carrot. Using the bottom half of the page, have your child count the number of carrots out loud. Explain that the number *1* means there is only *one* shown. Have your child color the number 1 and the carrot. ***Skill:*** Understanding the number 1.

Name ______________________________

Two

Directions: Using the top half of the page, show your child the number 2. Explain that Baby Daffy is looking at *two* ants. Using the bottom half of the page, have your child count the number of ants out loud. Explain that the number *2* means there are only *two* shown. Have your child color the number 2 and the ants. ***Skill:*** Understanding the number 2.

NAME ______________________________

THREE

3

3

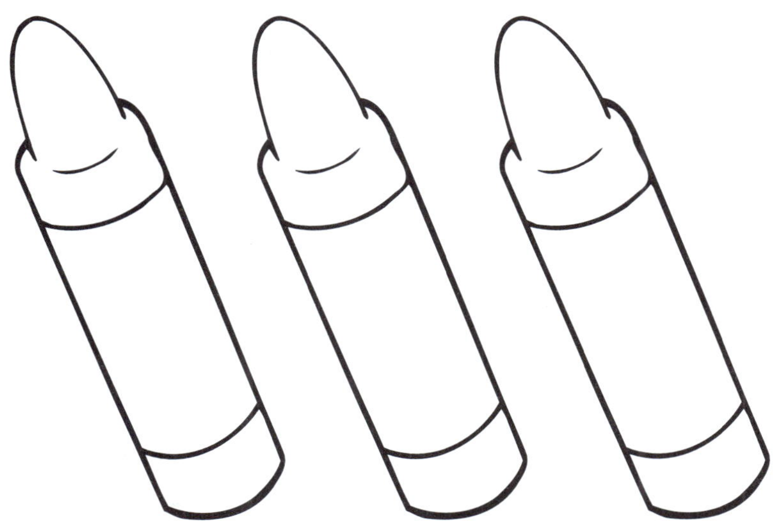

Directions: Using the top half of the page, show your child the number 3. Explain that Baby Tweety is holding *three* crayons. Using the bottom half of the page, have your child count the number of crayons out loud. Explain that the number *3* means there are only *three* shown. Have your child color the number 3 and the crayons. ***Skill:*** Understanding the number 3.

NAME ______________________________

Four

4

4

Directions: Using the top half of the page, show your child the number 4. Explain that Baby Elmer has *four* hats. Using the bottom half of the page, have your child count the number of hats out loud. Explain that the number *4* means there are only *four* shown. Have your child color the number 4 and the hats. ***Skill:*** Understanding the number 4.

NAME ____________________

FIVE

5

5

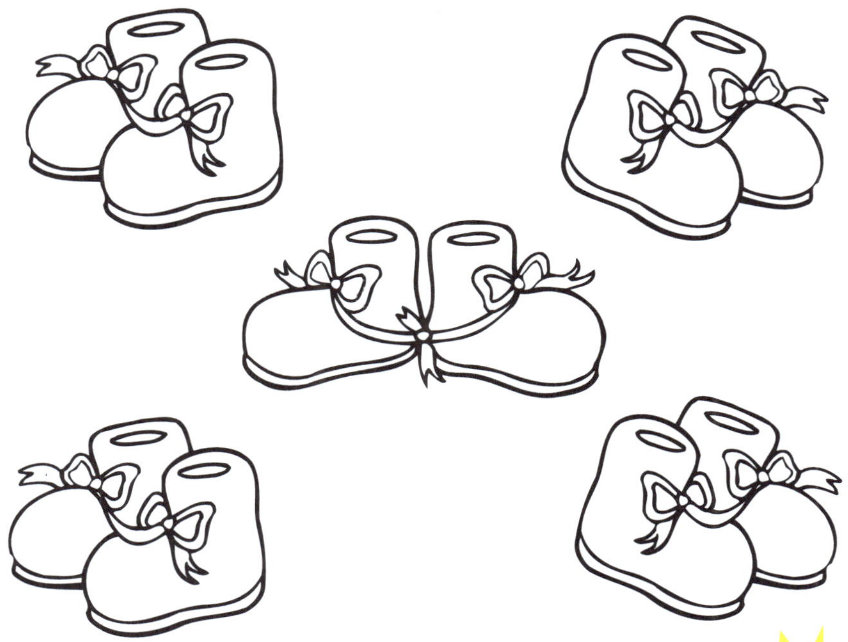

Directions: Using the top half of the page, show your child the number 5. Explain that Baby Wile E. is surrounded by five pairs of booties. Using the bottom half of the page, have your child count the pairs of booties out loud. Explain that the number *5* means there are only *five* pairs shown. Have your child color the number 5 and the booties. ***Skill:*** Understanding the number 5.

NAME ______________________________

SIX

Directions: Show your child the number 6. Explain that Baby Road Runner has pulled *six* feathers out of the pillow.
Skill: Understanding the number 6.

NAME

Six

Directions: Have your child count the number of feathers out loud. Explain that the number *6* means there are only *six* shown. Have your child color the number 6 and the feathers. **_Skill:_** Understanding the number 6.

NAME ____________________

SEVEN

Directions: Show your child the number 7. Explain that Baby Taz is looking at *seven* baby bibs on the clothesline.
Skill: Understanding the number 7.

NAME ____________________

SEVEN

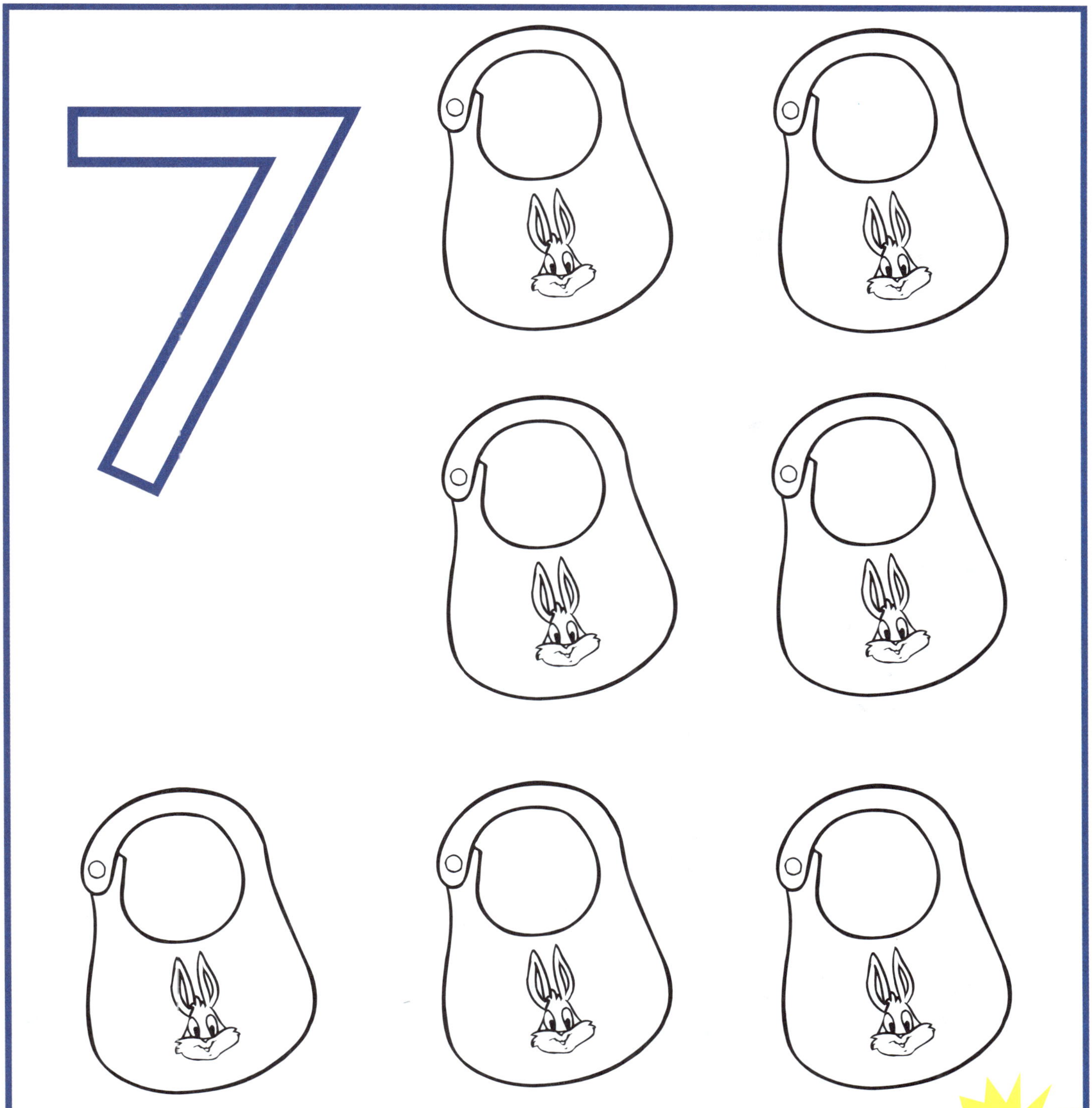

Directions: Have your child count the number of baby bibs out loud. Explain that the number 7 means there are only *seven* shown. Have your child color the number 7 and the baby bibs. ***Skill:*** Understanding the number 7.

NAME ________________________________

EIGHT

Directions: Show your child the number 8. Explain that Baby Lola is looking at *eight* pairs of roller skates. ***Skill:*** Understanding the number 8.

NAME ______________________________

EIGHT

Directions: Have your child count the pairs of roller skates out loud. Explain that the number *8* means there are only *eight* pairs shown. Have your child color the number 8 and the roller skates. ***Skill:*** Understanding the number 8.

NAME ____________________

NINE

Directions: Show your child the number 9. Explain that Baby Sylvester is surrounded by *nine* Baby Tweety blankets.
Skill: Understanding the number 9.

NAME ________________________________

NINE

Directions: Have your child count the number of blankets out loud. Explain that the number 9 means there are only *nine* shown. Have your child color the number 9 and the blankets. ***Skill:*** Understanding the number 9.

NAME

TEN

Directions: Show your child the number 10. Explain that Baby Speedy is surrounded by *ten* pacifiers. ***Skill:*** Understanding the number 10.

NAME

TEN

Directions: Have your child count the number of pacifiers out loud. Explain that the number *10* means there are only *ten* shown. Have your child color the number 10 and the pacifiers. ***Skill:*** Understanding the number 10.

NAME

ONE

1

1

Directions: Using the example at the top of the page, explain that Baby Bugs has *one* pie, and the number *1* means there is only *one* shown. Have your child count each group out loud, then circle the picture with *one* pie. Ask your child to color the number 1. ***Skill:*** Counting to 1.

NAME ______________________________

Two

2

2

Directions: Using the example at the top of the page, explain that Baby Daffy has *two* baby rattles, and the number *2* means there are only *two* shown. Have your child count each group out loud, then circle the picture with *two* rattles. Ask your child to color the number 2. ***Skill:*** Counting to 2.

Name

Three

Directions: Using the example at the top of the page, explain that Baby Tweety has *three* mallets, and the number *3* means there are only *three* shown. Have your child count each group out loud, then circle the picture with *three* mallets. Ask your child to color the number 3. ***Skill:*** Counting to 3.

NAME

FOUR

4

4

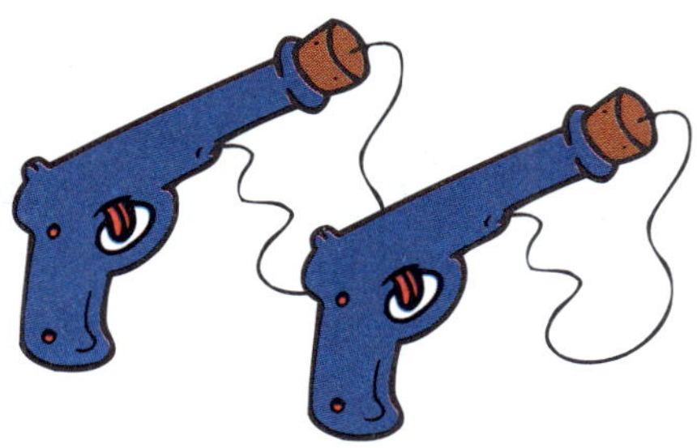

Directions: Using the example at the top of the page, explain that Baby Elmer is playing with *four* Baby Bugs dolls, and the number 4 means there are only *four* shown. Have your child count each group out loud, then circle the picture with *four* dolls. Ask your child to color the number 4. ***Skill:*** Counting to 4.

NAME

FIVE

Directions: Show your child the number 5. Explain that Baby Wile E. is playing with *five* tricycles, and the number *5* means there are only *five* shown. ***Skill:*** Counting to 5.

NAME

FIVE

Directions: Have your child color the objects, then count each group out loud. Ask your child to circle the picture with *five* tricycles. Have your child color the number 5. ***Skill:*** Counting to 5.

NAME

SIX

Directions: Show your child the number 6. Explain that Baby Road Runner's tricycle has *six* horns, and the number *6* means there are only *six* shown. ***Skill:*** Counting to 6.

NAME

Six

6

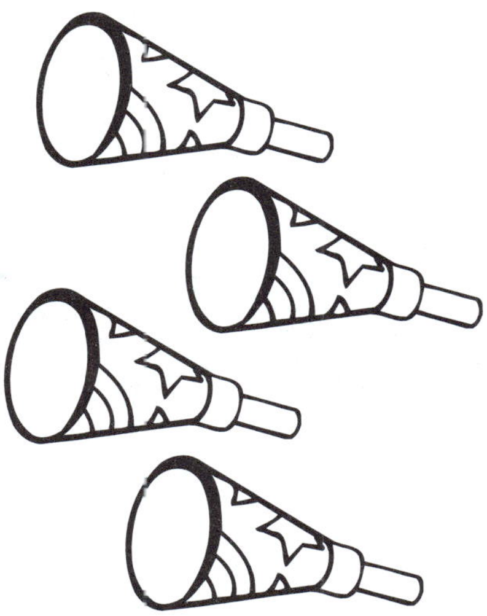

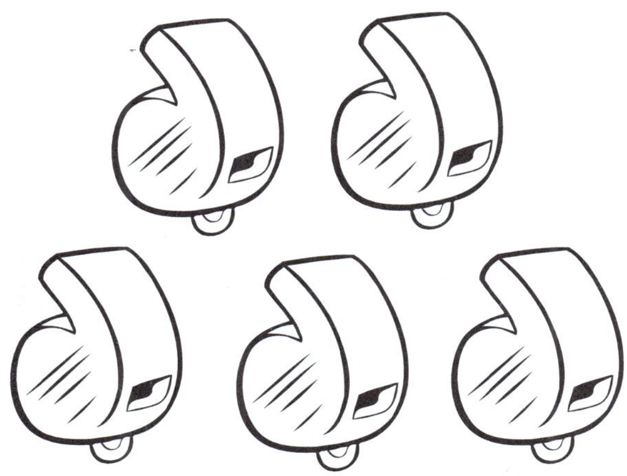

Directions: Have your child color the objects, then count each group out loud. Ask your child to circle the picture with *six* horns. Have your child color the number 6. ***Skill:*** Counting to 6.

NAME ______________________________

SEVEN

Directions: Show your child the number 7. Explain that Baby Taz is playing with *seven* tops, and the number 7 means there are only *seven* shown. ***Skill:*** Counting to 7.

NAME

SEVEN

Directions: Have your child color the objects, then count each group out loud. Ask your child to circle the picture with *seven* tops. Have your child color the number 7. ***Skill:*** Counting to 7.

NAME

EIGHT

Directions: Show your child the number 8. Explain that Baby Lola has *eight* hair bows, and the number *8* means there are only *eight* shown. ***Skill:*** Counting to 8.

Name ______________________________

Eight

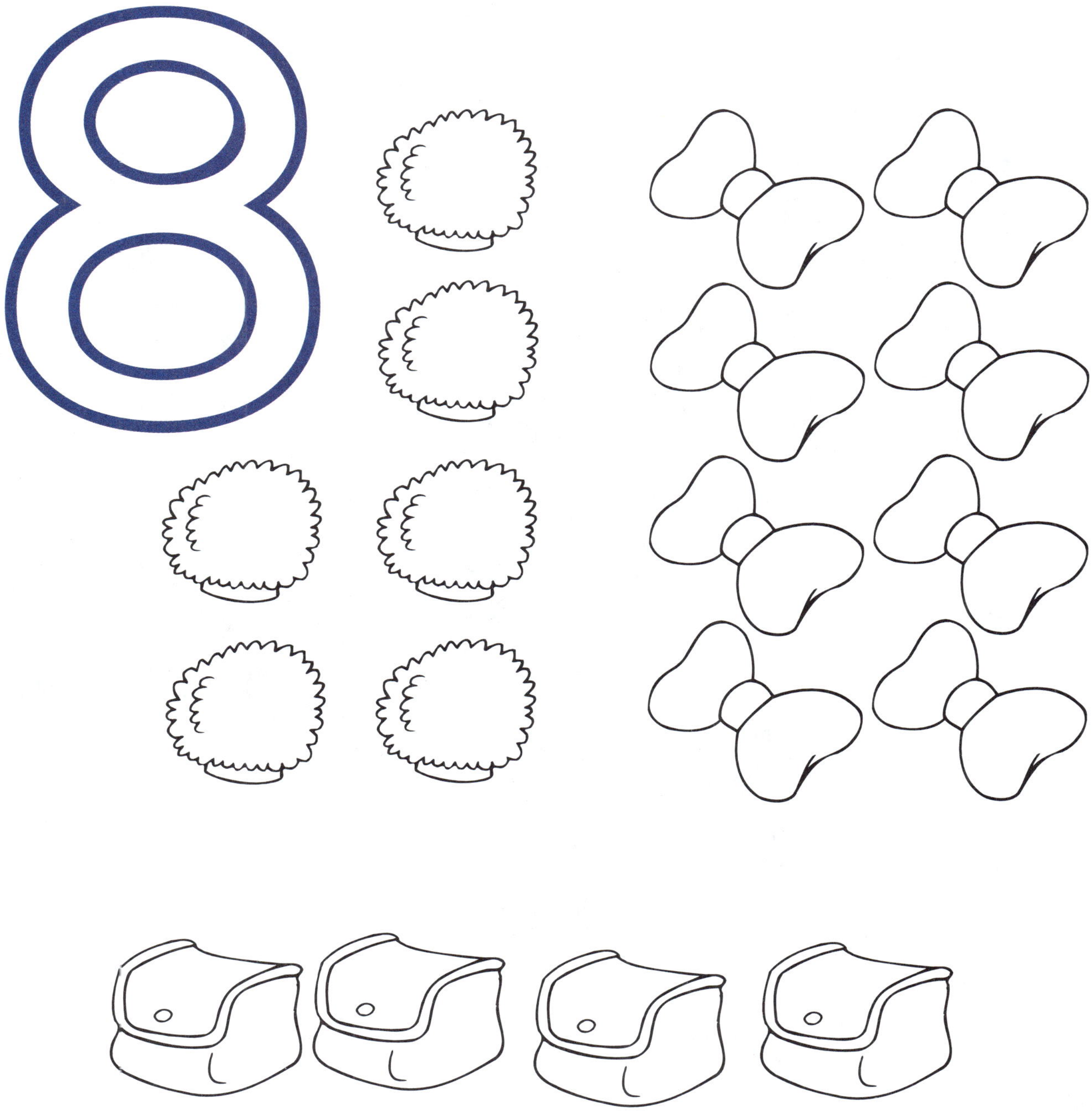

Directions: Have your child color the objects, then count each group out loud. Ask your child to circle the picture with *eight* hair bows. Have your child color the number 8. ***Skill:*** Counting to 8.

NAME

NINE

Directions: Show your child the number 9. Explain that Baby Sylvester is looking at *nine* lollipops, and the number 9 means there are only *nine* shown. ***Skill:*** Counting to 9.

NAME ____________________

NINE

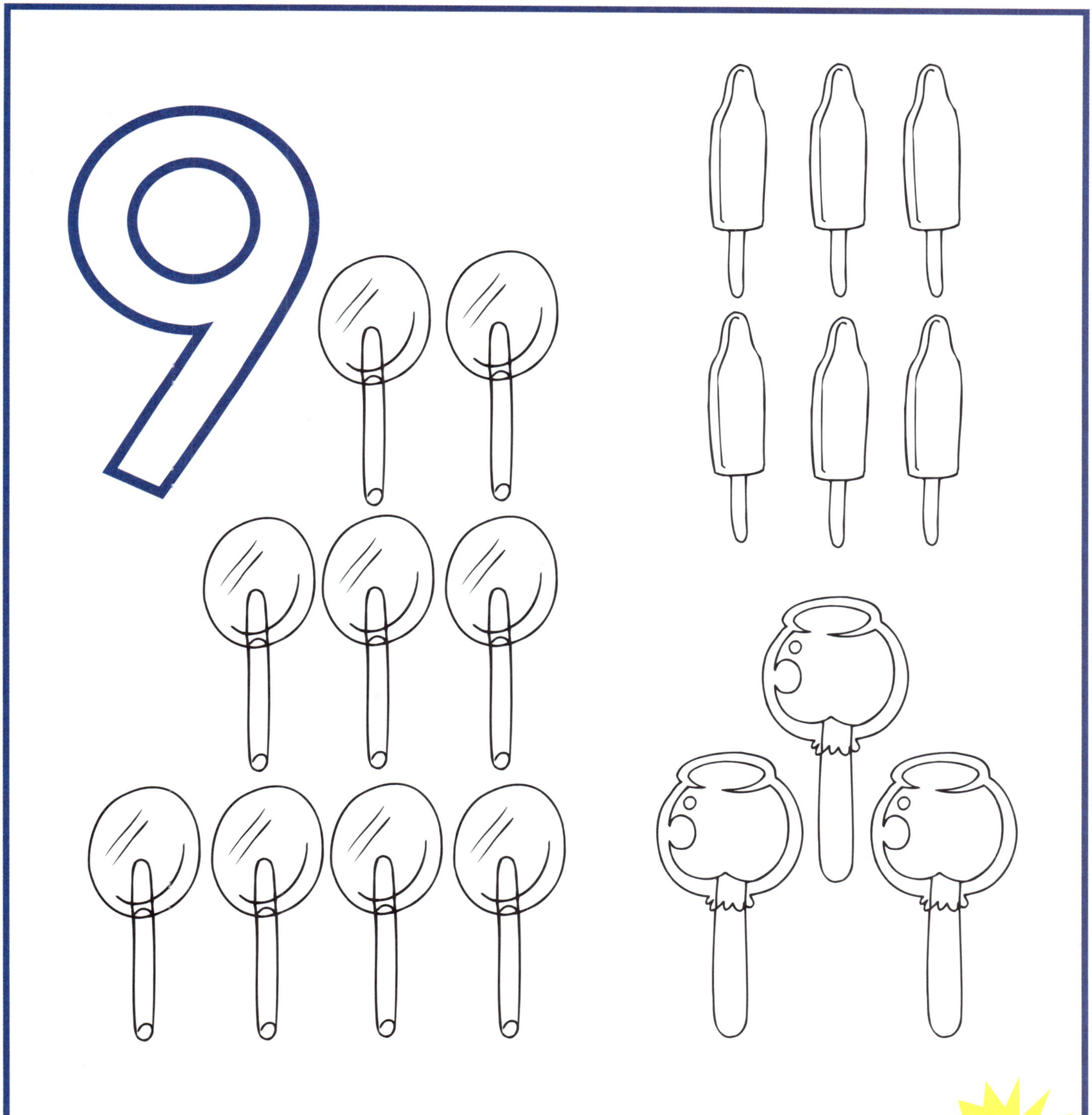

Directions: Have your child color the objects, then count each group out loud. Ask your child to circle the picture with *nine* lollipops. Have your child color the number 9. ***Skill:*** Counting to 9.

NAME ______________________________

TEN

Directions: Have your child count the Baby Looney Tunes characters. Explain that the number *10* means there are *ten* Baby Looney Tunes shown. Have your child color the number 10. ***Skill:*** Counting to 10.